This W Scale

41 Plays From The Drift Marketing Team To Help Your Business Cut Through The Noise, Grow Faster Than The Competition & Thrill Your Customers

By **The Drift Marketing Team**

Foreword by Mike Volpe, CEO of Lola.com, former CMO of Cybereason & HubSpot

Authors:
Dave Gerhardt
Daniel J. Murphy
Sara Pion
Alex Orfao
John DeWolf
Janna Erickson

Designed by Algert Sula
Edited by Gail Axelrod

CONTENTS

Foreword

By Mike Volpe
CEO of Lola.com
Former CMO of Cybereason & HubSpot

$15 million in Series A funding before they had a product.

An additional $32 million in Series B funding only 18 months from the launch.

Another $60 million in Series C funding in just two years.

150,000 businesses using the platform.

1 new product every month.

Drift is killing it.

And it's not just because they have an experienced founding team, a customer-driven culture and a great product.

Today, those things should be table stakes.

And while there are many factors that have contributed to Drift's hypergrowth, a key driver has been their unusual approach to marketing.

Instead of spending all their time looking at dashboards and worrying about funnel metrics, the Drift marketing team has focused on creating great experiences.

Instead of adopting aggressive lead generation tactics and desperately trying to push potential buyers down a funnel, they've treated people as people, rather than leads.

Instead of worrying about whether or not something will scale, they've focused on doing marketing that doesn't feel like marketing.

And by caring more about conversations than conversions, they've been able to build an emotional moat around the company.

For a new startup to break out the way they have in this day and age is inspiring.

And in this book, the Drift marketing team will share their secrets on how to grow your business with 41 seemingly unscalable plays.

Introduction

By The Drift Marketing Team

We talk a lot about role models at Drift.

Brands, thought leaders, marketers, artists, copywriters, entrepreneurs – people of all walks of life that inspire us. People we want to be like. People we want to learn from.

But there is one role model in particular that inspired us to write this book.

Marc Benioff, the Chairman, CEO and Founder of Salesforce.com.

And it's not just because Marc is a great CEO, a billionaire entrepreneur or because he's donated hundreds of millions of dollars to charity – although we admire him for that too.

Rather, it's because Marc is radically transparent in telling the Salesforce.com story so that others may learn.

At Drift, we are obsessed with learning.

When you walk into our office, you'll notice a giant bookcase filled with books. Take one, they are free.

One of our first one hundred hires at Drift was our Director of Learning and Development. That's very uncommon for such a small team.

Even our podcast, it's not called "The Drift Podcast" or "Conversational Marketing." Nope, it's called Seeking Wisdom. Because that's what we're all about.

In 2009, Marc Benioff published *Behind the Cloud: The Untold Story of How Salesforce.com Went from Idea to Billion-Dollar Company-and Revolutionized an Industry*. The book, an instant classic and bestseller, has been read by hundreds of thousands of people around the world who want to learn how one of the fastest growing companies of all time did it.

Marc gives candid advice, shares secret strategies and tells the story of how Salesforce.com grew from his apartment in 1999 to the leader of a $46 billion industry in just ten years.

While Drift is still in its early days, we don't want to wait years before we share our secret plays that have helped us grow. Like Marc, we want to be radically transparent.

Today, Drift is one of the fastest growing companies in SaaS history (a business model Marc and Salesforce.com practically invented).

Our company has been called "a reality show" instead of a "vendor" by Silicon Valley strategist Andy Raskin because our marketing is personal instead of corporate.

We've been accused of being **too good** at taking over our target audience's LinkedIn feed when we launch a new product.

And this year, at our annual conference, HYPERGROWTH, the fastest growing marketing and sales conference in the world, we had over 6,000 attendees in just our second year hosting it.

And as Mike Volpe noted, one of the reasons we've grown so fast is our unorthodox approach to marketing.

It all started with our founders: Elias Torres and David Cancel. They wanted to approach marketing differently. And then came Dave Gerhardt, now our VP of Marketing and co-host of Seeking Wisdom, who has taken their vision and made it real.

Together, they've redefined startup marketing, brand building and PR.

While most B2B startups are obsessing over scalability and tracking, Drift is not.

That's why we decided to pause from our day-to-day marketing operations and write this book.

While reading it, you'll discover not only our abnormal approach, but also hear never-before-told stories and learn how to implement our plays into your own marketing strategy.

This book is written exactly like *Behind The Cloud* in that it's 41 plays organized into chapters. We did that so you can put this book on your desk and thumb through it when you're looking for inspiration. That's often what we do with the books we read.

We hope you enjoy this book, we really enjoyed writing it. At the end, you'll find our email addresses and we'd love to hear what you thought of it.

– The Drift Marketing Team

Chapter 1
Start Marketing Before You Have A Product

Play #1
Don't Believe In Stealth Mode

When our CEO David Cancel (a.k.a. DC) and CTO Elias Torres founded Drift in 2014 they didn't have a product.

They had an idea, a few things in the works and a small team of engineers and designers who were beginning to lay the groundwork for a marketing and sales platform.

And while they were slowly letting customers in to test the alpha and beta versions of Drift (Driftt — with two ts at the time), they knew full well that the product wasn't going to be launched until at least a year later.

Most companies call this stealth mode — and it typically means that they operate behind the scenes without telling the world about what they're doing until an official launch date. In fact, many of them won't even let beta customers into the product before their code is flawless, the interface is pixel perfect and their website feels like Apple.com.

But DC and Elias made a conscious decision to start marketing before they started selling. And long before they had even set a launch date for the product, they hired Dave Gerhardt as employee number 10 and the first full-time member of the marketing team.

That was the first of many unconventional things we did at Drift to achieve what we call hypergrowth — or as

Alexander V. Izosimov defines it in Harvard Business Review:

> *"the steep part of the S-curve that most young markets and industries experience at some point, where the winners get sorted from the losers."*

And in the next 40 plays, we'll explain how marketing has helped us get there.

Play #2
Own The Demand, Not Just The Supply

The reason why DC and Elias decided to invest in marketing early on goes back to two fundamental beliefs that we share here at Drift.

One: You can only achieve hypergrowth by being close to the customer — and that doesn't just apply to the product and customer success teams but every single part of the company, including — if not especially — marketing.

As DC explains in his book (also called *HYPERGROWTH*):

> *"Every company in the world will tell you they are customer-driven. They'll believe in the principle. They'll even have framed posters on the wall about it. Solve for the customer.*

> *But none of that means anything unless you actually*
> *make the structural decisions to ensure it."*

But while Drift was built customer-first, we soon realized that being close to the customer is no longer enough.

And that led us to the second point: Instead of owning the supply, you need to own the demand.

If you look at the world around you, you'll notice that it's companies like Airbnb, Uber and Amazon that are winning today. Not only because they've been able to get closer to the customer than their traditional competitors like hotels, taxi companies and department stores, but also because instead of owning the supply, they own the demand.

We realized that in a world of infinite supply, the customer has all the power.

And that's when we knew that having the best product isn't enough. Having the best brand isn't enough. And having the best service isn't enough. It's the combination of those three things that will help us stand out.

And if we were truly going to solve for the customer, we had to invest in all three from the start.

Here's how we got started with the marketing piece of the puzzle.

Play #3
Find Your Wedge

While we were nowhere near having a product when Dave joined Drift, we had something better: a thorough understanding of the market that we would eventually enter.

But as anyone who's worked in the field of SaaS knows, we couldn't just say that we were going to sell to people in marketing and sales. That's far too broad in a crowded market like ours.

We needed to find our wedge within those fields – this one role that our product could serve.

And since we knew that Drift was going to sit on top of our customers' websites, we needed to talk to the people who controlled it — the people who could literally log in to the website's back-end and copy/paste the code to install Drift.

That's how we were able to rule out sales. Even though we knew that our product would have a big impact on leads, opportunities and pipeline, sales teams couldn't implement Drift on their own. They would need help from marketing.

Narrowing it down to marketers got us one step closer. So we started thinking, *"Okay, who in marketing could actually do this?"*

And that's when we landed on product marketing as the initial segment to go after.

That was our wedge.

Back then, all of us at Drift including DC, Elias and Dave had worked with companies that had a product marketing function. And the product marketers were the ones who were most likely to do what we call a "drug deal" — make a change on the website or inside of the product without having to tell anyone or get it approved.

So that became our focus — how do we get inside the minds of product marketers? How do we get close to them? How do we get them to think about Drift?

And that set the stage for the next three plays: Do your homework, go hand-to-hand and build an audience.

Play #4
Do Your Homework

Back in the early days, our product manager Matt Bilotti, Elias and our designers would do a bunch of customer research and customer development work.

Their mission was to talk to as many product marketers as possible to try and understand what they wanted from the product, what annoyed them about their current tech stack and how we could make Drift work for them. They were in search of pain.

It was through that search of pain that we found gold — and it had nothing to do with a feature in the product at all.

We learned first-hand that product marketers feel underserved and like no one knows exactly what they do. They wanted to feel some love.

So we thought we could start creating content for them — we figured, what if we started shedding more light on the role of product marketing? What does a day in the life of a product marketer look like? How do they define their role? What do they care about? What would they want to read, follow and share?

So we decided to focus our first marketing efforts on product marketers. We wanted to fill a gap in the market and create the content they had been missing.

What if we could get 10 product marketers to love Drift?

If we could get 10, we knew we could get to 20. If we could get to 20, we could get to 50, 100 and beyond. Product marketers will begin to tell their friends and other product marketers — and help us reach what Seth Godin calls "sneezers." Because when they sneeze, everyone else gets the germs — a.k.a. learns about Drift.

At the time, we didn't have any content on our blog yet. And we didn't have a podcast. So we decided to launch a newsletter — we wanted to send a weekly email with the best product marketing content from around the web. We could curate articles, videos, podcasts and all types of content focused on product marketing.

That was the idea for the newsletter — but we had no subscribers and we had no traffic.

So we needed to start collecting email addresses and building up our list by hand. One name at a time.

And that brings us to the next play.

Play #5
You Must Fight Hand-To-Hand

To get the first subscribers to our newsletter, Dave started combing through LinkedIn and Twitter, searching for people doing product marketing and sending them personal messages that went something like this:

> *"Hey. I'm starting a newsletter just for product marketers. We're curating the best product marketing content from around the web — from podcast interviews to videos to blogs. I thought you might dig it — and also have a few stories of your own to contribute. Can I send you a link to subscribe?"*

And sure enough, one by one the subscribers started to trickle in.

By the way, the key to that message above is asking for permission. The conversion rate is so much higher when you treat someone like a human and ask permission first vs. just sending them a link and begging.

From there, we started to get some amazing product marketers on the list. Our pitch also got better because we could use social proof when reaching out to other marketers:

> *"Hey, we started this newsletter for product marketers. People from companies like Twilio, Shopify, Dropbox and Marketo are all on it, we thought you might like it too."*

At Drift, we call this approach hand-to-hand combat. And it's the secret to how we got our subscriber base started.

And later on, we used the same tactic to get a thousand people to attend our first-ever HYPERGROWTH conference (and even to get 6,000 at our second conference in 2018).

There hasn't been one magic email that we sent that sold hundreds of tickets. Nobody just wakes up, comes to the website and buys.

No magic bullet. No growth hacks. No shortcuts. Just offering people something that we thought they might find valuable — and going hand-to-hand to make sure they got it.

Play #6
Build An Audience Early

The funny thing about hand-to-hand combat is that it actually helped us scale. Most of the product marketers we contacted were happy to hear from us — some of them even started contributing their own content and suggesting articles we should be sharing.

It was through these relationships with product marketers that we started to hear one thing over and over: Everyone had a different definition of product marketing.

So we decided to turn that into a piece of content. We figured that if people were having trouble defining the role, we should do it for them.

That led to Dave doing a few interviews, pulling from the customer research and writing a post that set out to define the role of product marketing and built around the number one thing people were typing into Google related to product marketing: *What Is Product Marketing?*

Largely because of that first seminal piece, we got our first ten subscribers. Then a hundred. Then a thousand. We had gotten into the minds of product marketers by creating a piece of content they could rally around and show to their friends and co-workers who didn't truly understand what they did.

As a result, our newsletter grew to a couple thousand people in our target market — before we ever even had a product to sell to them.

Even today, three years after it was published, that post still ranks number one on Google for the keyword *Product Marketing* and brings 5,000 new unique visitors to our website every single month.

All of that from one blog post written two weeks after we started officially "doing" marketing.

To make a long story short (and you can probably see where this is going), we ended up creating more and more content for product marketers, expanding beyond a newsletter to build a Slack group and a blog with weekly product marketing content.

And ultimately, we became this valuable resource for people — before a product, we had an audience.

So when we were finally ready to launch the product, we had an audience to announce it to.

We built a community that we could turn to and say, *"Hey, can I tell you about Drift?"*

People got to know us, trust us and get value from us long before we had anything to sell to them. We bridged the gap from being a complete stranger to being someone they trusted, so when we were ready to sell, they were ready to listen.

And so instead of having to go out and start building trust, all we had to do was tell our audience why they needed the product. We were able to skip the part where we'd have to somehow convince them to choose us.

Instead, we could focus on closing our first paying customers.

All because we had started marketing before we had a product, because we hadn't operated in stealth mode and because we had gone out and started a conversation with the right people at the right time.

And to this day, the biggest mistake we see startups making is waiting for the perfect time to start marketing.

We'll let you in on a secret: There's never going to be a perfect time. And here's another one: It's never too early to start marketing.

Chapter 2
Invest In Brand

Play #7
Bet On Brand

One of Dave's responsibilities as the first marketing hire at Drift was to start building the brand.

Unlike a lot of companies in the SaaS space, we weren't all that worried about the immediate ROI of our marketing tactics. We took a bet on brand because we believed that in the long run, we'd benefit more from telling an authentic and consistent story than all the one-off marketing growth hacks combined.

Beyond that, we had another good reason for going against the grain.

You might have seen Scott Brinker's famous martech landscape slide.

Known as the Martech 5000 — nicknamed after the 5,000 companies that were competing in the global marketing technology space in 2017, it's been said to be the most frequently shared slide of all time.

And already by early 2018, Brinker had updated it with almost 2,000 more vendors — that's nearly 7,000 marketing software companies fighting for the same buyers' attention.

While a lot of founders would argue that there's no point in

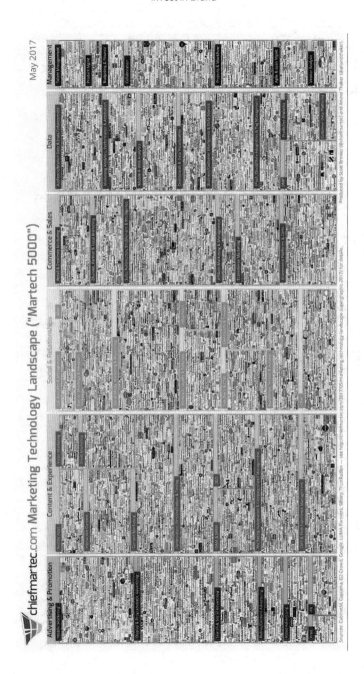

chiefmartec.com Marketing Technology Landscape ("Martech 5000")

May 2017

Management · Data · Commerce & Sales · Social & Relationships · Content & Experience · Advertising & Promotion

Produced by Scott Brinker (@chiefmartec) and Anand Thaker (@anandthaker)

Sources: CabinetM, Capterra, G2 Crowd, Google, LUMA Partners, Siftery, TrustRadius — see http://chiefmartec.com/2017/05/marketing-technology-landscape-supergraphic-2017/ for details.

even entering such a crowded market, DC and Elias took a different approach.

In fact, DC has this pretty unorthodox view on markets — he prefers those with a fair number of competitors. According to him, that's the best way to know there really is a market.

And so DC and Elias weren't going to get paralyzed by competition because they knew that where there's competition there are buyers. And where there are buyers there's money. And where there's money, there's an opportunity to achieve hypergrowth.

But the trick here is that you can't enter a crowded market and then do things like everybody else. Instead, we entered a crowded market knowing that we were going to focus on something that a lot of SaaS companies hadn't. We were going to build a brand.

As DC explains in a blog post called the Hypergrowth Curve, every successful company goes through the same three stages of evolution.

Let's use the marketing and sales software market as our example:

In the first stage known as the Edison Stage, companies can compete on commodities. All they need to win is a better product.

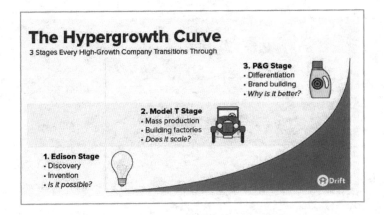

However, as the market matures, scaling up production becomes a priority. And so in the Model T Stage, companies must learn to deliver consistent quality at scale.

In the third and final stage, known as the P&G Stage, features and mass production capabilities won't get you very far. To compete, you need a brand to differentiate your company from the competition.

And since we entered the B2B SaaS market at a time when it was already swarming with competitors, we knew that to win, we would have to bet on brand.

In the following plays we'll show you exactly how we did that.

Play #8
Create An Emotional Moat
Around Your Brand

Before we get to the tactical stuff, let's take a moment to define what we mean when we talk about brand.

Because it's not just your logo, your tagline, your content, your ads or your charismatic CEO.

Sure, all those things are a part of your brand identity, but your actual brand is much more than the sum of all those visual and verbal cues. Your brand is the combined experiences a person has when they interact with your product and your company.

It's the emotional moat that makes them want to work with you instead of a competitor.

As Slack CEO Stewart Butterfield explains:

> "... even the best slogans, ads, landing pages, PR campaigns, etc., will fall down if they are not supported by **the experience people have** when they hit our site, when they sign up for an account, when they first begin using the product and when they start using it day in, day out."

That emotional experience is your company's brand — and

as Salesforce CEO Marc Benioff argues, it's your greatest asset:

> *"A brand is a company's most important asset. A company can't 'own' its facts. If the company's facts (speed, price, quality) are superior to the competition, any good competitor will duplicate them or improve on them."*

To build that moat around your company, you can't just pay a talented designer to create a brand identity deck and call it a day.

You need to craft a consistent story, where every touchpoint, from an ad to a blog post to a podcast episode to an email to the product, builds on the same core values and adds to the experience.

So while at Drift our titles and job descriptions on the marketing team may be similar to our colleagues in other SaaS companies, the "why" behind our work is different.

Instead of only focusing on how many views a new piece of content is going to get, we also make sure that it will help our customers and potential customers have a better experience with us.

And while we track the number of page views, unique visitors and clicks just like everyone else, we also understand that today all that information is free. People can find out everything they need to know about your company without ever talking to anyone at your company. The rules have changed.

And our goal with content is not to squeeze every click and lead out of it but to spread our brand as far as possible and make our content free and easy to share. Because when our content gets shared, our brand gets shared — and this way, people are more likely and willing to do business with us when they're ready to buy.

In the next few plays, we'll look at some of the tactics that have been the most pivotal to building our brand.

Play #9
Find A Channel The Competition Can't Copy

The difficult part about building a brand today is that there's more noise than ever, there's more competition than ever and buyers are more skeptical than ever. Every company has a blog. Every company is on social media. Every company is making videos. Every company has a podcast.

As consumers, we've learned to tune out marketing that feels like marketing. We want to be in control. And we never want to feel like we're being sold to. And let's be honest — the last thing any one of us wants is more content from some company.

This is exactly why we focused on building a brand at Drift. We needed to cut through all that noise, build real relationships, become the brand of choice for B2B marketers who were ready to buy and make ourselves available to start conversations with people live on our website.

One perfect example of that is how our podcast Seeking Wisdom has turned into one of our the best channels for brand **and** demand generation.

But it didn't start out that way.

When we first started the podcast it was just Dave's way of trying to get content out of DC. After all, a lot people in the SaaS space are looking for founder-level content, but it wasn't every day that we could get our CEO to sit down and write a blog post (if you're a marketer, you know exactly what we mean — CEOs often have the best content; it's just *impossible* to find time to get the content out of them).

And while originally Dave thought that he would just interview DC, get the audio and ghostwrite his ideas into a blog post, the interviews morphed into these two-way conversations where two people at different ends of their careers would talk about personal and professional growth.

DC – the 5-time founder and OG who's sold a bunch of companies and Dave, this young guy in his marketing career trying to figure out how he can grow and take the next step at Drift.

And that's what Seeking Wisdom became all about. That's what it still is today.

The reason we think it's been so successful is that it's such an authentic and real channel. And we end up with people from all over literally walking around with us in their ears. But there's no script — it's just two people talking about what's going on at Drift, books they've read, things they've learned and more. And there's very little editing. It's more of a documentary than a piece of marketing content.

The podcast has allowed us to be ourselves in front of all these people.

Play #10
Be You

If you've listened to Seeking Wisdom, you probably know that we love books and learning from others.

In fact, all the meeting rooms in our Boston office are named after our favorite authors. Even the lobby is full of their books — copies and copies and copies, free for our guests and employees to grab on their way out — from *Ogilvy on Advertising* to *Shoe Dog* to *Influence* (we'll show you all of them when you come visit our office).

But before joining Drift, most of us in the marketing team

had been working in SaaS and doing marketing at other software companies, so we had followed all of the typical marketing advice from around the blogosphere that focused on tips, tricks and hacks — like how to improve your email open rate or how to get more clicks on your Facebook ads.

But from the beginning, DC gave us some pretty controversial advice: Stop reading SaaS marketing blogs. There will always be a new tip, trick or hack to figure out — and that stuff comes and goes. But there's one thing that has **never** changed in marketing: people.

DC pushed us to focus on the timeless lessons in marketing and to really dig in and understand copywriting, human behavior and social triggers. And when he suggested that we ditch the marketing blogs, he had a good point.

For example, if one study came out that said the best time to send an email was Tuesday at 2 PM, guess what most B2B marketers would do? They would start sending their emails on Tuesdays at 2 PM.

So we flipped it and started studying the classics. Instead of spending all our time learning about things that we're going to change tomorrow, we went back in history and studied the classic branding, advertising and copywriting books to focus on learning all these timeless lessons about the things that don't change.

And there was one thing that stood out from all of those

books: The best way to win customers and build a brand is to be you. To be real. To be authentic. To be human. And that lesson has been true for hundreds of years — but it's even more important today with all of the noise and competition in the market.

So from the way we write to the kind of images you'll see on our website (a.k.a. no stock photos), everything comes back to this: We have a set of brand values that drive everything we do here at Drift, and they are all about being **us.** And that means being real, being authentic, being human — and at times even exposing our flaws to the world.

Instead of trying to act like somebody else, we've spent all this time being ourselves. We've spent our time on doing marketing that feels more authentic, more human and more approachable.

And if there's one channel that has allowed us to do this, it would be video.

Play #11
Use Real, Authentic Video

In *Let My People Go Surfing: The Education of a Reluctant Businessman*, Patagonia founder Yvon Chouinard shares the secret behind Patagonia's one of a kind brand that has stolen the hearts and minds of consumers all around the world:

> *"Our branding efforts are simple: Tell people who we are.*
> *We don't have to create a fictional character like the*
> *Marlboro Man or a fake responsible caring campaign like*
> *Chevron's "we agree" advertising. Writing fiction is so*
> *much more difficult than nonfiction."*

It's harder to write fiction than nonfiction.

That quote says everything about how we think about brand at Drift, and that's exactly why we love video as a marketing channel, because when it comes to being authentic and real there's no channel quite like video. You just can't fake it. And there's nowhere to hide.

When we talk about video, we usually mean scrappy, low production stuff with minimal editing and no script whatsoever. Sure, we have the high production videos too — but the biggest lever for us has been real, first-person video shot on an iPhone.

This is the reason why channels like Instagram and Snapchat have blown up: Because people want the real life, reality TV — not always the highly manicured videos. But even though Snapchat and Instagram sound obvious, not a lot of brands — especially in the B2B space — have understood the value of authenticity and copied that style for their marketing.

What these companies are missing out on with their expensive productions and professional scriptwriting is the ability to show everyone out there what's going on behind the scenes.

Be it B2C or B2B, people buy from other people. And that trust is a lot easier to build if your audience can see your face and hear your voice.

That's why we also use a lot of video in our sales and marketing emails. It doesn't have to be perfect and it definitely doesn't have to be expensive.

It's just our way of saying: "Hey, you're talking to real people and not just some faceless corporation. We're here if you need anything." Video is one of the most authentic forms of marketing there is today.

One of the best examples of this is what we did with our pricing page. We were getting a lot of comments and questions about an early version of our page that was leaving people feeling confused and lost. We made numerous revisions of the layout and copy on the page, but still didn't make any progress — so we turned to video.

We were going to have someone on the Drift marketing team explain pricing in the video, but then we had a better idea: Let's have Will Collins do it. Will is the VP of Operations at Drift, and his team is in charge of our pricing. So we got him on camera to explain pricing because we figured if he can't explain it clearly, then who can?

Marketing is everyone's job inside of your company, and video makes this easier than ever (more on that later too).

Play #12
Get Rid Of All Your Stock Photography

Showing our faces is actually one of our brand values.

And what we mean is that everything we publish needs to have a real face on it. And so we even have a landing page checklist that enforces the rule: You can't ship it until it has a face.

And not just a stock image of a random person, but a real Drift employee or customer — that's the rule. No stock photos.

The reason why we're so bullish on real faces is simple: It

makes our brand more human.

But it wasn't just stock photos that we ditched — we got rid of cartoons and animations in our content as well.

Even though our designers would create these cool blue, white and gray cartoons and animation-like illustrations for our blog posts, landing pages and social media channels, we realized there was nothing distinctively "Drift" about them. They didn't feel real. They felt like, well... cartoons.

Sure, they were nice to look at and even quite funny at times, but they were images that any other brand could've created quite easily. Besides, they did nothing to reflect our core values.

So one day, we just decided to forget about stock photos and these cartoony illustrations and go for something that was perfectly on brand: real pictures of real people. Drift customers or people who work at Drift. That's it.

At the end of the day, we want all our marketing to feel like you're talking to a trusted friend; someone you know and want to talk to — not a colorful illustration or a complete stranger and especially not a faceless corporation.

So whether they were photos from events we hosted, or photos from team outings, or just photos of us working in the office, we gathered them all up and started using them on the blog. And today, we hire a photographer to come to our office once a quarter to take more photos of us being us.

Customers sometimes get on a video call with their customer success manager for the first time and go, *"Oh, do I know you from somewhere?"* — and that just make it all the more real. We want that.

So if you're looking to make your brand feel more human, this is the easiest place to start: Add real faces to everything you do.

Chapter 3

Build A World-Class Marketing Team

Play #13
Master The Marketing Fundamentals

Before we discuss hiring and developing a world-class marketing team, let's talk marketing fundamentals.

Because, as we see it, there's a problem with marketing today that goes beyond strategy or the tools we use.

DC was right — in many ways — when he said that marketing has lost its way.

Marketers are too fixated on the technology to help them do their job, and not nearly focused enough on the actual marketing.

Dan saw this first hand and has referenced this as his "rebirth" into marketing when he arrived at Drift.

After a few months of working at Drift, Dan realized there was a whole other part to marketing that he hadn't even scratched the surface of.

Things like writing amazing copy. Designing a beautiful advertisement. Or constructing messaging and positioning your product — where the true talent in marketing lives.

See, we have a marketing culture at Drift.

We celebrate great ad copy — any collection of words that

Daniel J. Murphy
@_danieljmurphy

Problem in marketing:

Marketer thinks "We bought something so I should get XYZ result"

Part of the problem is over hype

But the bigger problem is that marketing has become a profession where we depend on tools and not our creativity

Are we just number crunchers or creatives?

8:54 PM - 26 Apr 2018

3 Retweets 43 Likes

♡ 5   ⟲ 3   ♡ 43   ᴵᴵᵎ

gets stuck in our heads.

We nerd out over emails that are so good, we write back to the author with kudos and sometimes, *"Are you happy at your current company?"*

Real marketing.

Our marketing culture is centered around learning. Dave pushed Dan — and the whole marketing team — to read books from the greatest marketers in the world — like how David Ogilvy approaches ad copy and Dan S. Kenney writes sales letters.

Those books have become the center of our approach to

marketing and we've even built checklists around them.

Like in *Influence: The Psychology of Persuasion* Dr. Robert B. Cialdini breaks down the psychology behind why people say *"yes."* There are six universal principles behind persuasion:

1. **Reciprocity** – pay back what we receive
2. **Scarcity** – people want what they can't have
3. **Authority** – people follow credible experts
4. **Consistency** – consistency with past actions
5. **Liking** – people say "yes" to things they like
6. **Consensus** – looking for what others have done

Dave printed out these six principles and has them taped to the top of his desk. That way every time he writes a new email or blog post he makes sure he hits all of them in his message.

Now all of us on the team do that. It's our recipe for writing great email, blog and landing page copy.

And that's the thing. Because it started with Dave outlining the fundamentals that were important for our marketing approach, we're able to hire and build on that foundation.

That's why it's so important to start with outlining your fundamentals before you scale the team.

Play #14
Make Marketing Everybody's Job

The best marketing channel that no one talks about is marketing internally to your team.

At Drift we believe that marketing is everybody's job — it's not just the people with *marketing* in their titles.

And if you think that everyone outside the marketing team understands what you do and is naturally inclined to promote the company's work to the rest of the world, you're dead wrong. Because the hard truth is that no one cares about marketing. And that's because too often they don't understand its value.

One of the most important parts of our job as marketers is sharing our work to the company and explaining why what we do matters.

In fact, when Dave first started at Drift and was asked to get up in front of everyone to share what he'd been working on, he could've easily just listed the things he did, like, *"I wrote a blog post and tweeted four times."*

Instead, he told a story. He explained that the way people buy in B2B has changed. Today, before even agreeing to meet with a salesperson, people like to read stuff online, listen to the company's podcast and check out their blog.

He explained how these pieces of content help build trust among the target audience. And since Drift didn't have a blog before Dave started, he told everyone that he had spent his first week writing the first post and getting the blog live on our website.

And that's exactly what internal marketing is all about: Getting in front of people and explaining why what we do matters to the rest of the company. And perhaps what they can do to help.

Because at the end of the day, if you can't get the people inside of your company to believe your message, how will you convince outsiders?

It's simple math, really: If you have a marketing team of three in a company of fifty people, wouldn't you rather have all fifty people making noise about the brand than just the three?

But while this makes perfect sense on paper, not many companies are investing in internal marketing. Either they don't understand what they're missing out on, they don't put in the time for it or they just assume that people will naturally contribute to marketing when they feel like it or have the time.

So at Drift, we try to bake internal marketing into everything we do and make it part of our weekly rituals as a company. The marketing team joins the weekly sales meeting at 12 PM every Monday, and the marketing team presents every Friday at 4 PM at our company *Show & Tell*.

And we take both of these opportunities as seriously as we would an external speaking opportunity because the mission is clear: Get people onboard with what we're doing.

If building marketing into our weekly meetings and rituals is the number one secret to internal marketing, support from the management team at Drift is number two. Without their unconditional support, it would be impossible to borrow a busy engineer for a quick video shoot, convince the whole company to tweet about a new product, or have everyone record LinkedIn videos on launch day.

Play #15
Let Go Of Your LEGOs

While internal marketing has helped us grow fast, it has also introduced a new kind of a challenge:

At a fast growing company like Drift, you can't afford to get territorial over your job. From day one, you need to accept that every single goal, task and output will be somebody else's responsibility soon.

As Molly Graham, a former Facebook, Google and Quip exec explained to us at a Lunch & Learn at the Drift HQ in

Boston: You need to be ready to replace yourself every 3 to 6 months.

> *"That is how you get the opportunities that no one should reasonably give to you... If you're willing to take these enormous leaps, and just be unafraid of what you don't know and be willing to learn."*

What she means is that your job isn't yours forever. At any given moment, you need to be ready to let go of your LEGOs and let the other kids (a.k.a. teammates) play.

Because here's the thing: The kind of hypergrowth we've been lucky enough to witness first-hand doesn't just happen to the company — it must be driven from inside the company. And in reality that means that every employee must be ready to take on new responsibilities and let go of old ones.

That's why we've made it our mission in marketing to learn as fast as we can.

Let's look at Dave for example. When he joined Drift back in 2015 as a Senior Marketing Manager, he was employee number 10 and the first marketing hire for a company that didn't even have a product yet. It was his job to define what marketing meant for Drift, and which channels and tactics the new function would consist of — and that meant he had to own everything from blogging to email to SEO to events to PR to paid marketing and more.

But as we grew, Dave grew too. And in the past three years, he's been asked to replace himself multiple times, hiring writers, video producers, product marketers and many others.

And it's not just Dave — we've seen the same exact thing happen with the other members of our team.

Dan has switched between product marketing, demand generation and then back to product marketing — all within a year. Sara transitioned from being a customer advocate (a support role) to join the marketing team and is now working on the Growth team. Alex has lead our email strategy, co-marketing and now is shifting into channel marketing.

So the bottom line is this: As easy as it is to get sucked into your current role and start manically defending it, the territorial model just doesn't work in a fast moving environment. Instead, you have to rely on your whole team to help you out and learn to look up and down the organization to execute on your goals.

And in the next play, we'll explain how we approach hiring new team members when the time comes.

Play #16
Forget About Pedigree

Here at Drift, we don't over-analyze whether a new team member is fresh out of college or the former VP of Marketing at a big name SaaS company. Regardless of their background, every new hire is given the same amount of respect and autonomy from day one — and they have one clear expectation when joining: Delivering results.

Instead of your resume, pedigree or former accomplishments, we care about the results that you get after joining the team. Almost everything resets after you join the team at Drift and you're expected to prove yourself in a new environment.

Because a common mistake that many fast growing companies make in building teams is that they take someone's track record at a different company as proof of their future performance.

But just because someone excelled in a previous role doesn't mean they'll be able to replicate that success in a new environment. And that's why we're very careful not to let our expectations or bias get the better of us.

When you join Drift, you need to start from zero and prove yourself from week one. Our culture is all about results, rather than the hours you put in.

But what results should you drive? To answer that question, we write 1/7/30 plans for each new employee. These outline what you should achieve in your first day, your first week and your first month at Drift. It's one of our most important checklists because it makes sure success is clearly defined for new employees.

We sweat over outcomes rather than outputs. And we'd much rather hire people with something to prove than those who already think they know everything. Rather than chasing big logos or over-emphasizing our candidates' resumes, we focus on finding people who can deliver results.

That's why we ask everyone to do a project with us before they even come in for their first interview. This filters the candidate pool because not everyone wants to do it — but the ones who are hungry to join Drift do it gladly. It also helps us get a feel of what it's like to work together and to see how someone thinks and operates.

Not everyone is going to pass that homework assignment. But it's always been a helpful part of the interviewing process. Not only will we learn, but so will the candidate.

At the end of the day, your performance matters much more than your pedigree.

Play #17
Create A Playbook For Getting Promoted

Hiring someone at Drift — regardless of their past experience — is only the beginning. After that, it's up to the new team member to prove that they can grow with the company.

And to make promotions as transparent as possible, we've come up with this internal 9-point checklist that we use to justify career progression:

1. To be considered for a promotion, you need to own a number. If you're in SEO it can be organic traffic, if you're in content marketing it can be website traffic and if you're in event marketing it can be the number of tickets sold. The important part is that everyone has a number and that they're committed to growing that number.

2. Speaking of ownership, you also need to own the area of marketing you're responsible for. No one will micromanage you and you'll get to figure stuff out for yourself. The catch, however, is that you'll also be accountable for that area. And so if something breaks, it'll be up to you to fix it.

3. Another thing we require you to do is to plan and forecast your own success. As a company, we have

some pretty lofty goals, but it'll be up to you to dream up yours — and then report on the results.

4. If we want to keep going after hypergrowth, and we do, we can't settle for good enough. So to get your next promotion, you need to constantly raise the bar in your current role. You need to make it difficult for yourself to find someone to take over your role. Only then are you ready to move on.

5. You also need to master your craft. Be it through video tutorials, books, role models or mentors, we're expecting you to be a leading talent in your current role before you move onto a new one. A part of this is creating systems and checklists to help the next person succeed.

6. To move forward in the company, you need to not only do your job well but also do it fast. You need to push the pace in every way that you can and forget about things that you think you know from your previous jobs. If it takes 4 months to build a new website somewhere else, you need to figure out how to get started with ours this week.

7. The highest performing members of the marketing team are experts at managing their managers. They run their own 1:1s and give their superiors alternative solutions to a problem instead of just asking them for a decision. Managing up is

key to taking the next step in your career.

8. Before you can be promoted, you need to become really open to taking feedback and putting it into action. You need to stop taking even the most difficult feedback personally, and become truly coachable.

9. Making your team successful is another trait that you'll need to hone before getting a promotion. Start by hiring and onboarding an intern, and helping them become successful.

This is more of an art than a science, but providing everyone on the team with a clear checklist helps guide conversations and gives everyone a path to at least have a conversation about the next step.

Play #18
Fail Fast, Learn, Don't Make
The Same Mistake Twice

Just as our promotion checklist suggests, the ability to move fast is absolutely essential if you want to build your career here at Drift.

This goes back to forgetting about our preconceived notions and being able to learn faster than the competition. It's not an ego-trip or a vanity thing, but rather a fundamental principle in the way that our marketing team operates.

We're not worried about failing, because just as Molly Graham taught us, *"It's not really a failure if you learn in the process of trying."*

Of course, not every new tactic will be more successful than the last. But since we make sure to learn from each experiment, at least we won't repeat the same mistakes again.

That's why an essential part of the learning process is documenting it. After a product launch Dan would write an "after action report" to document how the launch went and specifically call out mistakes or issues.

Each month's after action report is reviewed early in the preparation process for the next launch. That way the marketing team would never make the same mistake twice.

Every launch will have problems. Some small, some large. So taking that report and specifically calling out the issues will force your team to correct their mistakes and get better in time for the next launch.

This process of putting failures under a microscope and examining them applies to every area of marketing, not just product launches. From website design to demand generation — if we don't properly assess ourselves, how are we supposed to get better?

Now, here's the thing. When taking this approach, you need to find balance. Your team can't write an after action report for everything you do in marketing. That's unproductive. The most important part is that your marketing team adopts the mentality. This must become part of your culture: "*A bunch of things went well, but here's how we can improve next time.*"

Chapter 4
Learn From Role Models

Play #19
Always Be Learning

If there's one thing that everyone at Drift shares, it's our collective commitment to learning new things. We're constantly looking to grow both personally and professionally.

It's something that David and Elias talk about a lot. It's at the very core of who we are as a company — and as a group of people. It's even in the name of our podcast: Seeking Wisdom.

On the marketing team, this obsession with learning is both a challenge and an opportunity.

It's a challenge because we're never going to be completely satisfied with an event we produce, a piece of content we write, or a tweet with two glaring typos (but so many likes we can't delete it).

And it's an opportunity because we can always go back to something that we've just published yesterday and go, *"Oh yeah, I can come up with at least 10 things I'd do differently if I got to do this all over again."*

So even though we know that we'll never be perfect, our work improves gradually. Every day, we're a little bit better than we were the day before.

And because we're each accountable for our own numbers, strategies and tactics, we're extremely committed to learning. We know exactly when we need to change course and try something new.

There are no blockers either because we have full ownership of our own results. And so if Dan is responsible for demand generation and he's not hitting the goals that he's set for himself, well... he'll just have to come up with a plan b.

But that doesn't mean that he'll have to execute on it alone.

Because the way we see it, learning is a team activity. That's why we're happy to help each other come up with better titles for our blog posts, write email copy for another teammate if they have too much on their plate and share feedback as much as possible.

Because at the end of the day, that's the only way to keep learning.

One of the easiest ways to learn in marketing is to ship daily. Just like our product teams are expected to ship daily, so are our marketers. Shipping is oxygen — and publishing new content, copy and campaigns is the quickest way to get feedback on something in the real world. So shipping daily has become a mindset for everyone in marketing too — but always be learning doesn't stop there. In the next few plays, we'll shed some light on what constant learning looks like in practice here at Drift.

Play #20
Keep A Swipe File

One of the most interesting things about being a marketer is that we're not only doing marketing but we're also being marketed to. Constantly.

And because we're naturally subjected to other companies' marketing on a daily basis, we've been able to create what we call "swipe files" — these secret stashes of screenshots, links and screen recordings that we store in Trello, Evernote or Google Docs for inspiration.

Sometimes it's great copy or an email, and other times it's a cool animated GIF that caught our attention — but the common denominator is that it's something we'd like to apply to our marketing.

Because as Dave likes to remind us, there's no point in reinventing something if you can just add on top of something that already exists. And it's something we talk about a lot: Instead of inventing something from scratch, go out and look for well known patterns that you can copy and innovate on.

Now, this doesn't mean *actually* copy something — but it means learn from what worked and what didn't.

For example, if we're creating a new set of ads, we'd go and study other brands and find things that they have done that have worked and then create the Drift version of them. Of course there are times when we need to invent something completely new, but most of the time, what we're trying to do already exists.

This way, when we're getting ready to write a blog post, shoot a video or design a new landing page, we don't have to start from zero — we can just go check out our swipe files to see if there's anything we could use as a starting point.

By constantly "swiping" what we see, we're able to write better copy, create better experiences and start more conversations. All because we're constantly taking in all these different examples from different industries.

Play #21
Find Mentors And Learn From Them

While swipe files are a great place to start when you need inspiration to hit fast, we're also big believers in learning from other people.

Normally, when people talk about mentoring, they mean long-term relationships with people who are 20-30 years ahead in their careers. And while formal structures like that can be hugely beneficial in terms of professional growth, they're not the only way to help you get ahead.

In fact, DC has pushed us to broaden our view of mentoring in three different ways:

First, somewhat similarly to the traditional model, DC has armed our marketing team with two external advisors: Mike Volpe and Tom Wentworth. These local industry OGs who come to the office to work with us, share their ideas and give us feedback on a regular basis.

These visits are extremely valuable to the whole team, because being able to share our content and numbers with them and getting individual feedback really pushes us forward. It makes us aspire to that next level and work even harder to get there.

Second, we're big on role models we don't necessarily know but from whom we actively learn.

That's why each person on the marketing team has at least a mental if not a physical list of all the people we're currently studying and trying to learn from.

One of the greatest things about these kinds of role models is that you don't have to commit to a long-term relationship with them like you normally would with a mentor. Instead you can — and should — keep changing them as you learn new things and progress in your career.

Third, we've realized that we don't need a formal mentorship program in the company to learn from our co-workers. We simply surround ourselves with smart people, listen to them and observe them as they do their work.

Not everything has to be a formal process. You can learn a lot without having to go far out of your way.

Play #22
Start A Book Club

When it comes to learning, books are a cheap and easy way to learn from people who you wouldn't normally get to learn from.

Think about it: Books allow you to expose yourself to whatever topics you're interested in, without forcing you to continue your relationship with them beyond what's useful

to you.

And that's why we created the Drift Book Club.

It's not a traditional book club where we all read the same book and get together to talk about it. Our book club is an online board where we can recommend books to each other, and then Drift will buy those for us.

By supporting our obsessive reading habit, the Drift Book Club helps us build a collective frame of reference and allows us to swipe the best lessons from the best thinkers out there.

The Drift Book Club consists of dozens of books already and it's growing each week.

Play #23
Learn From People You Don't Like

"We're all biased. Most of us only want to learn from people we like or want to be around. And that's a huge roadblock to growth. Because most of the people in the world are not perfect. So if you're waiting around for someone you like — someone that's perfect — then you're going to be waiting for a long time."

– David Cancel on episode #129 of Seeking Wisdom

It's easy to get trapped in one perspective and feel certain that that perspective is right. And it's hard to listen to a perspective you don't agree with.

Maybe it's a YouTube star you don't really like – but they have a massive audience. If you want to grow your brand's YouTube channel you should study how they grew their audience. Just because you don't like them doesn't mean you can't learn from them.

It's not always easy. And just like you, we're biased too. Recognizing that bias has only helped us grow faster.

Whether it's a thought leader or a brand we don't see eye-to-eye with, we still listen to their speeches, watch their videos and read their books.

Chapter 5

Create A Category

Play #24
Use The First-Mover Advantage

When we were just starting to build out the marketing team, there was this one book in particular that we borrowed from: *The 22 Immutable Laws of Marketing* by Al Ries & Jack Trout.

And according to the very first law, called the Law of Leadership, it's better to enter a market first than to do it later with a better product. But since we were entering a space that was swarming with 5,000+ competitors, first-mover advantage wasn't exactly in the cards for us.

And so we had to resort to law number 2: The Law of Category, which suggests that it's better to create your own category than to try to compete in a crowded one.

What's important to note here is that market and category are two distinctly different things. While marketing software is a market, inbound marketing would be a category. And the category doesn't have to be radically different from the market — just different enough.

Think light beer versus imported light beer and you've got the difference.

Now, a lot of people don't know this but we spent two years trying to come up with a name for our category. We can't even tell you how many conversations we had with the team trying to come up with something that would accurately describe what we do.

The truth is that when we finally came up with *conversational marketing*, DC didn't even like it at first. But because we committed to it and made a point of using it, it only took our customers a couple of weeks to pick up on it. They started saying it back to us.

And then a month later, we started to see non-customers tweet about it.

Fast forward a few more months, and the term was everywhere. Hundreds of companies around the world were talking about it, major publications were writing about it,

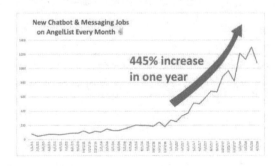

An email from May 2018 that Angelist sent to 4.5 million subscribers about conversational marketing.

competitors were starting to use it and we owned it.

In the spring of 2018 the number of jobs in conversational marketing had quadrupled from the previous year according to AngelList.

And that's when we knew we had something.

Play #25
Stand For Something

Another book that we borrowed from in the early days was *Play Bigger: How Pirates, Dreamers, and Innovators Create and Dominate Markets* by Al Ramadan, Dave Peterson, Christopher Lochhead and Kevin Maney. It talks about how all the companies with the largest IPOs in the past decades have gone out and created their own categories.

But the trick here is that the category can't just be about the company — it has to be about something bigger.

So instead of only talking about Drift, we also spend a lot of time trying to grow the category of conversational marketing.

That's why we started the Conversational Marketing University (cheap plug: drift.com/university) and that's why we wrote the book on conversational marketing (cheap plug #2: drift.com/book).

And these are just two recent examples. We do all kinds of things to educate people about conversational marketing and to help them understand why it matters. We do it because we firmly believe that when the category grows, people will associate it with Drift. And eventually, they will come back to us.

But the problem is that having a category isn't enough — you also need a movement. You need a cause. Something to stand for.

One of our favorite examples of this comes from Salesforce:

When Marc Benioff founded Salesforce, he created a new category: Cloud-based CRM. But he also needed a hook — something that would get people interested in the category.

And so together with his team, he started a movement known as *The End Of Software*.

At the time, *The End of Software* movement was attractive, because it promised to free companies from clunky software, on-premise servers and annual contracts. It simply offered them a more flexible way of buying and using a CRM.

And because the pain points of traditional software were so widely accepted, it wasn't difficult to convince people to jump ship.

Taking a page from Benioff's book, we chose our cause.

Known as the *No Forms* movement, we publicly swore off lead forms and started promoting a more conversational way of marketing and selling.

What we didn't know then was just how big the whole thing would become. But as it turned out, a lot of marketers had spent a long time cursing lead forms. No one had just gone out and said it out loud before.

And while the *No Forms* movement was definitely bigger than Drift, we were able to reach a lot of people and get them interested in the category first and then the product. All because we had a shared enemy: Poor user experience.

Play #26
Start A Movement

Another important lesson that we took from the Salesforce playbook goes back to organizing events. And not just webinars or local user groups, but also big conferences that give us the opportunity to meet our customers and prospects face-to-face.

But instead of opting for a traditional sales and marketing conference with 45 minute keynotes from fellow Boston SaaS folks, we decided to do something different.

Again, we wanted the event to be bigger than us. Bigger

than marketing and sales. Instead of a traditional event or a conference, we wanted to create a movement.

And it had to feel "Drifty."

So in April of 2017 we announced HYPERGROWTH, a one-day conference with 15-minute features from inspiring authors, entrepreneurs and business leaders — and not only your usual suspects, but also people from the health, fitness and food industries.

HYPERGROWTH is not a conference where you'll learn the top six ways to optimize your Facebook ads, the top ten SaaS onboarding growth hacks or even the best practices for building chatbots on Drift. It's nothing like that.

It's a conference about personal and professional growth. And that's why it's called HYPERGROWTH and not the Conversational Marketing Conference, or the ConMarCon or the CMC.

Play #27
Give It A Name

Speaking of names, you're probably starting to notice a bit of a pattern: We're pretty big on naming things.

The Hypergrowth Curve, hand-to-hand combat, Seeking

Wisdom.

Just like every one of our landing pages needs a face, we don't rest until every event, every framework, every concept and every video series has a name.

And there's a very good reason for why we do this: To become real, things need a name.

If you go back and listen to the early episodes of Seeking Wisdom, you'll notice that David is always dropping these metaphors and stories. After a while, though, we realized that none of our listeners knew how to reference those afterwards, because — you guessed it — we hadn't given them names.

And while spending those precious extra minutes, hours and sometimes even days on coming up with a great name for an individual piece of content may seem like a colossal waste of time to some, we've actually found it super helpful.

And what we've learned over time is that the name doesn't have to be perfect. And not everyone has to love it at first. It just needs to stick.

Play #28

Welcome Competitors Into Your Category

I know that sounds weird, but welcoming competitors is the best way to scale your category.

Because here's the thing: While you want to own it, having your competitors in your category actually validates its legitimacy.

Here's the perfect example.

Look at Uber and Lyft.

While both are giant multi-billion dollar companies today, there's one underlying distinction between the two competitors.

Uber is the *verb*.

Uber was the groundbreaking first ride-hailing service launched in March 2009. It was first.

When people describe ride-hailing (even when ordering a Lyft) they'll say "I'm going to Uber home."

That's why Uber is valued at $48 billion and Lyft at only $15 billion.

But here's what people don't talk about: It's because Lyft

entered their category, that Uber grew so fast.

If you look at Uber's valuation over time, it skyrocketed from $346 million in February 2012 to $3.7 billion in August 2013. That's 10X growth.

What happened in those 18 months?

Lyft launched in June 2012.

Chapter 6

Start
Conversations

Play #29
Talk To Your Customers

When people ask us why we're betting on 1:1 conversations at a time when everyone else is obsessing over automation, volume and scale, our short answer is this:

20+ years ago marketing was all about getting the messaging right, opening the door to sales and starting a conversation. But then something happened. We got all this cool new technology — and so we over-rotated. As an industry, we got too excited about contacts and MQLs.

As a result, most companies started treating people as leads instead of people. And with marketing automation, they could just push this faceless mass to click on a CTA and fill out a form without ever even talking to them.

But these companies had forgotten something very important: Conversations drive the business. After all, a sale doesn't get made until a conversation happens.

And so the only "growth hack" we've ever actually given away in our blog is this: Talk to your customers.

Yup, that's right. No magic tricks or hard science.

Find out their likes, dislikes and pain points. Ask them about their hopes, fears and desires. Because even if you have a great product, nobody's gonna buy it unless you can demonstrate its value to them. And you can't demonstrate the value until you understand what drives your audience to buy.

And while you're at it, you can also kiss your no-reply email addresses, self serving Twitter monologues and pre-recorded webinar presentations goodbye. Because from now on, your only job as a marketer is to drive conversations.

Play #30
Optimize For Conversations

The number one email marketing metric we track is conversations — not clicks.

Sure, we also keep an eye on our open rates because obviously we want people to actually read the emails. But what we really want is for people to reply to us so we can have a conversation with them.

That's why our marketing emails come from our real email addresses. You'll never get an email from no-reply@drift.com or even marketing@drift.com — nope, you'll get them from Alex, Sara, Janna, Dan, Cody, Chris or Dave.

In addition to having a real human being as a sender, every single one of our emails also has a PS — a little call to action at the very end, typically a question like: *"One favor before I go: reply to this email and let me know why you signed up?"*

And you know what the crazy part is? People actually reply. In fact, the response rate to this email is something like 40%.

We also make a point of replying to every single one of these emails. We try to be helpful and answer any questions we're asked.

And while we know not everyone who replies is ready to buy, we do everything we can to leave a positive impression.

That way, down the line if and when they realize that they need a conversational marketing platform, they'll know who to ask first.

But since this book is all about sharing our secrets, we're gonna let you in on a pretty big one: We weren't always great at email. In fact, when we were just getting started, we were honestly quite bad at it.

> Hey there -
>
> I just wanted to send you a quick note to say thanks for joining our newsletter and set some expectations.
>
> Well, okay just one expectation: you should expect this email to be helpful every week. If it's not, we want to hear it from you. Tell us on Twitter @DrifttHQ or reply to this email.
>
> If you love customers as much as we do, then I think we're going to get along just fine :)
>
> There isn't a great email dedicated to the folks that market to customers, so that's what we're setting out to do here.
>
> **A Few Things To Get You Started for Week 1**
>
> 1. Slack is awesome. Product marketers are awesome. So we decided to combine the two and make a slack channel. Click here to get access. Once you're in you can share what you're working on, ask questions or just send a few emojis - that's cool too. Help us make this community awesome.
> 2. Why do people like the CEO's of Slack, Buffer and Help Scout care so much about customer success? Find out here.
> 3. We shared five examples of brands that are experts at positioning on our blog this week. See why we think they have product marketing down to a science.
> 4. If you want to see Twitter founder/CEO Jack Dorsey as a punk skater and read about 10 amazing entrepeneurs who accomplished nothing by the age of 30, you need to read this.
>
> Ok that's it for now. We'll see you next week.
>
> - Dave Gerhardt (@davegerhardt)
>
> **PS.** Feel free to share great links you've read at any time. Just reply here.

An email from the early days of Drift Marketing sent by Dave to our newsletter subscribers.

As you can see from the example above, back then we couldn't pick just one thing we wanted our new subscribers to do. We asked them to do a total of six different things: To tweet at us, to join our Slack group, to check out three different pieces of content and to reply to the email. All in one message.

It's no wonder this email didn't do all that much for us.

But what we learned from the underwhelming results and a few great benchmarks was this: In email marketing, you need to be very clear about what you want.

Hi, friend!

(Note to self: Start collecting email first names...)

Well, this is an exciting moment, at least for me: You have now subscribed to my newsletter! Thank you!

I hope it's an exciting moment for you, too: Not as exciting as a new puppy or a birthday, perhaps. But a modest thrill nonetheless.

I post on my site weekly-ish. (Emphasis on the "-ish.") You'll get a notification that looks like this (but with a teaser and link to the new content) whenever I publish something new.

In the meantime, I'd love to hear your answer to this one question:

Why did you subscribe to my site? What do you hope to learn here? Your answer helps me to know you a little better, so that I can offer you real value in return.

Again, I'm glad you are here. Don't hesitate to drop me a line at ann@annhandley.com whenever I can help you.

Thanks again. And welcome!

Ann

Here's a clear call-to-action from Ann Hadley's newsletter subscription email. It asks for a conversation rather than a click.

With examples like this as our guiding light, we were able to tweak the welcome email.

And over the course of the next 12 days, we received 75 direct replies from real people telling us how they found Drift, why they signed up and what they're working on. Without even having to look at the stats, we knew that we were onto something.

So the real lesson in all of this is that email works much better when you've picked the one thing you want people to do.

For us, that one thing was — and still is — conversations. And so we only optimize for them.

Play #31
Make Live Webinars Interactive

If you've attended a lot of webinars, you've probably noticed that most of them are not very conversational in nature. In fact, a lot of times you might as well just watch the webinar recording afterwards, because there's minimal interaction between the host and the audience.

But if you ask us, the best thing about live webinars is that they're... well, live. And so we try to make them as conversational as possible with a few simple tricks:

First, the best webinars we've had so far haven't been scripted. There are no slides and no formal agenda. Just two people talking to each other about a topic that they both know well.

Second, at the beginning of every webinar, we say hello to the the attendees by name. We want to build a relationship with them and make them feel like they're a part of a bigger community of like-minded people.

The bottom line is that we want the webinar to feel like a conversation. We want all the attendees to leave the webinar with their questions answered and having learned something new.

Play #32
Make Conversations On Social Media A Priority

Early on, we made a promise to ourselves that we'd reply to every tweet, Instagram Story, and LinkedIn comment we'd get.

We still do that.

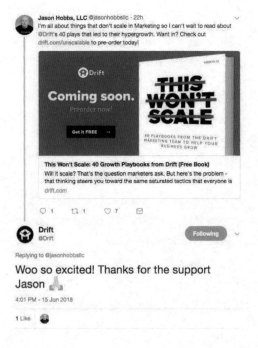

And we do it because we want everyone to know that we're real people. We want them to know that our responses are not automated and it's not just some bot, but us — real people from the Drift marketing team.

Trust us, it's not easy — when there are a million other things our team needs to get done — to prioritize tweeting... It's really not easy. You can't get in front of your board of directors and say leads were down but we replied to every tweet last month.

But luckily we've never had that issue. And we've never had to try to quantify how replying to a tweet impacts our business. We know from the conversations we've had and the feedback we get that it's worth prioritizing.

Conversations are always our priority.

And as we've learned over the last few years, it's not just on social media where conversations should be a priority.

Play #33
Kill Your Darling Forms

It's no secret that B2B marketing has been running on gated content and lead forms for the better part of the past decade.

And in early 2016 when David called Dave to suggest that we take down all our forms, Dave's initial reaction was terror. Back then, lead forms were our go-to lead gen tactic after all.

How the hell else are we going to get leads? was the one question that was spinning around in Dave's mind.

But before Dave even got a chance to disagree, DC had already launched into an explanation:

> *"I think marketing has kind of lost its way a little bit,"* he said.

> *"We've lost the importance of a great story and truly connecting with people. We live in this world where it's all about content, content and more content. And SEO. And ranking for this keyword and that keyword. And algorithms and conversion rate optimization. Pieces of that stuff are still important to marketing, but overall, I think we've lost our way. Marketing today has become more about gaming the system and get rich quick schemes."*

And that's when Dave realized something: Successful SaaS brands like Slack and MailChimp had never made people jump through hoops in exchange for value.

In fact, he couldn't remember ever filling out a form on either of those brands' websites apart from when he'd signed up for their products.

And here's why: Slack isn't winning because they were able to get more people to fill out lead forms than HipChat. MailChimp isn't winning because they were better at lead nurturing than Constant Contact.

They are winning because they have built amazing brands that people actually want to work with — and amazing products that people want to share with their friends and colleagues.

And if we wanted to win, we knew that we needed to stop asking people to jump through hoops.

Right then and there we realized that we needed to take marketing back to its roots and kill all our lengthy lead forms for good.

We decided to build a billion-dollar business by creating things that people actually want — not by tricking people into filling out forms just so we can email them to tears until they either buy something or unsubscribe forever.

Chapter 7

Write Better Copy

Play #34
Write Like You Talk

By now you've probably noticed that we're not fans of proper grammar, punctuation or big words.

That's because we made a very deliberate decision years ago to write the way we talk. All our blog posts, emails, social messages and other content are written this way. Even this book.

We do this for two reasons:

First, marketing writing only has one goal: To make people care.

People have short attention spans and no patience. If they don't understand something immediately, they move on. That's why we care more about being understood than having perfect grammar.

Second, we want our writing to feel like a conversation. After all, our product is a conversational marketing and sales platform and our main goal is to help people connect.

To do that, we can't just talk to our buyers — we need to talk **with** them. It's a two-way conversation.

That's why everything we write should feel like an email from a friend. It's not necessarily witty or well versed. It's not an academic paper or an article in The New York Times. And it definitely shouldn't sound like we needed to pull out a thesaurus to write it.

No, it's nothing like that. When we write something, we simply want you to get what we're saying, why it's important and what you can do about it.

We may have missed a comma but if we can help somebody understand, we've already won half the battle.

Play #35
Spend Time Getting Your Headlines Right

Most people can spend several days writing a 10X blog post. They'll read through it over and over, rewrite some parts and rephrase sentences. And when they're done with all of that, they take thirty seconds to write the headline.

That's not us. We obsess over headlines at Drift.

In fact, pretty much every one of us on the marketing team has felt the same initial confusion, surprise and concern when we've first realized how much time and effort goes into writing one headline.

It's like how can a small marketing team get anything done

when they spend so much time on these tiny details? And on something as trivial as a headline?

But here's the thing. We all chime in on headlines because we know just how important they really are.

Especially in a space as crowded as sales and marketing where there's already so much noise we need our headlines to stop people in their tracks and make them go, *"Damn, I want to read that."*

Of course you've gotta back up the headline with great content. But without an amazing headline you would have a readership of zero.

That's why we have Slack threads with over 50 messages bouncing headlines back and forth. Dave will give his feedback, then DC will chime in. So will Dan. And then others.

We write 10-15 variations of every headline and then kick them around with the team until we finally find one that we really like.

So if you're reading this book to find quick wins or practical tips, here's one: You've got to spend time on the headline. It's the only way to get people's attention online.

Play #36
Opt For Plain Text Emails

If you subscribe to our emails, you know we don't use email templates. And this too has to do with grabbing our audience's attention.

We actually ditched highly designed html marketing emails a long time ago. Even before we stopped using lead forms to gate content.

And here's why.

In a book called *The Boron Letters*, Gary Halbert explains that people tend to sort their mail into two piles: You've got your A pile and your B pile.

The B pile is where all those colorful flyers and ads end up. Basically anything that looks like it's from a brand.

The A pile is a stack of handwritten white envelopes. The A pile is personal. You'll know there's a letter from your Aunt Mary because you recognize her handwriting and know that every year she sends you 20 bucks for your birthday.

You always start from the A pile. More importantly, you read all of those letters.

You might eventually get to the B pile or you might just

throw it out. You weren't expecting any of that stuff and you definitely wouldn't be upset if some of the mail in your B pile got lost in the mail.

At Drift, we want all of our emails to end up in the A pile.

We want them to feel like it's your Aunt Mary asking you out to lunch this weekend.

And that's why we write our marketing emails just like we write any other email. We just open Gmail and start typing.

We don't care about proper punctuation. Sometimes our subject lines are all lowercase. And you'll never see us send an email with a pretty blue background, the Drift logo, a nice gradient and a big button that reads *"click here to read more."*

When you get one of those emails with fancy colors, logos and gifs, something goes off in your brain and you instantly know that it's an email from a brand. It's pretty, but you know it's an offer or a promotion.

And no matter what — whether you immediately delete the email or continue reading it, you're biased because you know the email has marketing intentions. And 99% of the world hates being marketed to.

Instead, we send scrappy plain text emails with lots of questions — and we actually want people to respond. We care more about starting conversations than optimizing for open rates and click throughs.

For example, when you subscribe to our blog, you won't get a traditional *"your subscription has been confirmed"* email.

Nope.

Instead you'll get an email from a real person. More specifically, Alex from our marketing team. Not from <u>no-reply@drift.com</u>.

And while she's quick to confess that the email is automated, she also writes, *"I'm a real person that would love to hear why you subscribed to our blog?"*

That's been an absolute game changer because we are creating a real connection with people.

These emails help us generate tons of feedback and allow us to start conversations.

Is it scalable? Hell no.

But we still do it.

Most marketing teams would debate whether or not to try that idea: Who would manage the conversations, how much time it would take away from that person and ultimately, how does it scale?

At Drift we just do it. We don't think about scaling. We'll try anything if we think it'll help us grow.

Play #37
Teach Every Marketer To Write For The Brand

Alex writes our emails, but she's not the only writer on the team.

The way we write is an important part of our brand. That's why every member of the marketing team is expected to write great copy.

It doesn't matter if you're an event marketer, a product marketer or a video producer — writing is everybody's job.

You don't need to be an English major and you don't need to have perfect grammar. You just need to write like you talk.

And while that may sound simple, every new hire in the marketing team has to go through intensive training and scrutiny on writing.

We believe in the power of feedback. And when a new member is brought onto the team we give them consistent feedback to get them where they need to be to be writing for the brand.

In addition to learning from the other members of the team, we also spend a lot of time studying some of the greatest direct response copywriters, marketers and ad gurus of all time. We basically use them as our copywriting role models.

We do this for two reasons.

First, these guys could literally convince anyone to do anything. After all, they knew how to get people to open their mail, read the mail, write a check, send it back and get the postage. Now compare that to what we have to do: Try to get people to click a link.

Second, you need to study the things that don't change.

Even though some of these books were written over a hundred years ago, the one thing that hasn't changed since the beginning of time is people.

So while we live in this fast moving world of SaaS where the technology and the landscape are constantly changing, we don't just obsess over funnel metrics or analytics. We obsess over people.

We need to understand our potential customers and buyers as people, not just some leads in our database. Like we said earlier, a sale doesn't happen until a conversation happens.

And after reading something like 6 of these books, you'll notice that these copywriters have one thing in common:

They understand people. So we read these books to learn the timeless lessons of emotions, desires and human behavior.

And that's our lesson. Forget the best practices. Forget what the SaaS bloggers are saying. Just go back and study these books:

* *Ogilvy On Advertising*, David Ogilvy
* *Scientific Advertising*, Claude C. Hopkins
* *Ca$hvertising*, Drew Eric Whitman
* *The Ultimate Sales Letter*, Dan S. Kennedy
* *The Copywriter's Handbook*, Robert Bly

Because if you understand what makes people move, you're gonna become a better marketer.

Chapter 8

Think Bigger With Your Product Launches

Play #38
Turn Your Product Launches Into A BFD

Product launches are a huge deal here at Drift. In fact, the entire company is organized around shipping a new product to our customers every single month.

Not just a bug fix or a new feature, but a completely new product.

Internally we call these product launches Marketable Moments. And if you follow us on Twitter or LinkedIn, you may already know that internal marketing is absolutely critical to their success.

All of our top website traffic days in company history came on Marketable Moments.

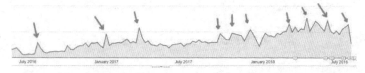

A snapshot from Google Analytics looking at www.drift.com web traffic since 2016. The arrows indicate product launch days (a.k.a. Marketable Moments).

One of our most successful product launches to date was in March 2018 when we launched Drift Email for Marketing.

And instead of just having our employees tweet and share a blog post on LinkedIn, we had everyone at Drift shoot and share a custom video on their LinkedIn accounts introducing the new product.

To get everyone excited and committed to shooting their own videos, we got in front of the whole company and told the story of how this could help us reach hundreds of thousands of people.

After that, Sara created a list of all our employees and went around the office asking each and every one of them whether they were going to take part.

On the morning of the launch, the videos were just our employees walking to work and talking to their iPhone cameras saying that we had just launched Drift Email for Marketing and explaining what's great about it.

That was until our product manager Alexa posted a video of her skiing somewhere in the Midwest, talking about the new product to the camera.

That was when all hell broke loose and everyone in the team started one-upping each other and posting all these different videos. Even the executive team got involved. Someone even shot a video asking a local barista about how he felt about marketing emails.

There was no link to Drift.com and even then, that was the highest traffic day to our website in the history of the company.

We didn't get paralyzed by tracking URLs or measuring the success of each individual video. Instead, we figured that if this was going to be as successful as we thought it would be, we could always just use high-level metrics like traffic and conversations to prove it.

In hindsight, it seems fair to say that we were right not to worry.

In fact, we received tons of feedback. Dave's inbox blew up. A recruiter got mad because for several days all he could see on his LinkedIn feed was Drift. Someone even made a parody video of Alexa skiing.

No matter how you look at it, the LinkedIn takeover was a success.

And ultimately there were three reasons for that:

First, we were able to take advantage of LinkedIn at a time when it was heavily weighting native video.

Second, we managed to go from idea to execution in less than a week because we have a small and agile marketing team that was ready to scrap our original plan and try something completely different.

Third, and most importantly, we have an amazing team here at Drift, and we got everyone on it to rally together.

Without the contribution and clever ideas of Alexa and all the people who followed her mark, we could never have reached a quarter million people in 24 hours — all without spending a dollar on promotion.

Play #39
Obsess Over Getting The Whole Team On Message

After the LinkedIn takeover a lot of people would reach out to us wondering how we got 100+ people to stay on message. Weren't we afraid that someone would say something stupid?

The answer of course was no. After getting people really excited about the new product, all we had to do was make sure they knew exactly how to explain its benefits to our customers.

And since we have a Marketable Moment every month, we've become quite good at ensuring consistency across different channels and the team.

Here's how we do it:

First, we make sure that everybody knows the details of the next Marketable Moment a month ahead of time.

Second, we don't just wait around to show our stuff in meetings, Friday afternoon Show & Tells and training sessions. We're also constantly sharing new graphics, copy and headlines on Slack and on our wiki to get people excited about what's going to happen.

Third, we use a tool called PostBeyond to share all the messages and materials with the team. Having a consistent system and a platform where everyone can access the same information at any time allows us to run successful social takeovers like the one we did on LinkedIn.

Fourth, and most importantly, we try to make all of this fun and exciting. By sharing our excitement with the team, we're able to turn them into a powerful marketing weapon. We get them to take the message and run with it.

Play #40
Over-Communicate Everything

Getting in front of your team once isn't enough. It takes much more than that to get them on board, on brand and on message.

That's why over-communication is vital to the success of our product launches. So much so, that it deserves its own play.

One of our inspirations here is Bill Belichick, the legendary head coach of the New England Patriots — and Dan's personal hero.

Bill is well known for winning year after year, even with new and often inexperienced players on the team. And one of the keys to his success is — you guessed it — over-communication.

At Drift, we've swiped this part of Belichick's playbook. Just like he's all about sweating the details and making sure that everyone on his team knows each play in detail, we've made sure that everyone at Drift knows our plays. So on gameday (launch day) there's no confusion about what each team member needs to do.

We're committed to making everyone an expert on the launch by holding meetings, repeat meetings, and sharing our headlines, timelines and follow-up campaigns.

We do it because every time, 5 new Drifters get excited about the launch.

And to us, every new team member represents a new LinkedIn profile and Twitter account that will help get our message out there.

Play #41
Build An Army Of Supporters Outside The Company

Every company has loyal fans. They love the product, the brand or the people.

But most companies haven't learned how to leverage these fanboys and fangirls for a product launch.

And if you ask us, that's a huge mistake.

Because these are the people who want to spread your message, hype up the new product and give you the referrals and third party validation you need.

And that's why we've built an army of external supporters known as the Drift Insider Network.

The network consists of some of our customers, advisors, investors and friends, who are naturally interested in hearing about what we're up to and happy to lend us a hand when we're about to launch a new product.

Much like internal marketing, it's critical to brief the insiders early on, go into some depth with the information and most of all, get everyone really excited about the new product.

A month before each Marketable Moment, we tell our Insider Network about what we're about to launch. We give them beta access, we use their quotes on our landing pages and we ask them to publish blog posts about our new products on the day of the launch.

Because as powerful as it is to have 100+ team members making noise, having external supporters make a lot of noise about your launch is even more powerful.

Final Thoughts

Data-driven and scalable.

Those are the two characteristics most B2B marketing teams today seem to strive for. And while there's really nothing wrong with either of the two, at Drift we have a somewhat unorthodox approach to both.

Being data-centric is good for the obvious reasons: Data isn't biased. It's factual.

It can help us set measurable goals and track our progress. It helps us figure out which tactics to double down on and which ones to forget about. It informs our decisions — but note the distinction here — it can never be the sole driver.

Because here's the thing: While data can be very useful, it can also be very dangerous.

And that's because data is inherently backward looking. It can tell us whether an existing tactic is working but it won't help us decide whether or when we should try something new.

It can make us believe that automation is the only thing worth doing. And when framed poorly, it can make it look like we're already doing everything we can to grow the business when in fact we're wasting all our growth potential on repeating the same thing over and over — only marginally better.

Second, the very reason why B2B marketers are so obsessed with data is its ability to tell us whether or not something will scale.

And that's quite natural, too. In a world obsessed with automation, volume and growth, it's no wonder that most marketing teams would ideally like their marketing tactics to be repeatable at scale.

But the problem with becoming obsessed with scale is that we forget why we're doing marketing in the first place. By becoming data-centric, we essentially lose out on our ability to be customer-centric.

And so while killing our lead forms and spending hours on a single headline may seem absurd, these seemingly unscalable things are in fact what have helped us grow.

Because instead of worrying about our numbers, we've been focused on people — and more specifically the kinds of experiences they have with Drift. In fact, just like our product team is building our platform with the customer at the center of their universe, the marketing team is doing marketing with the customer at the center of ours.

By talking to people instead of staring at spreadsheets all day, we've learned that people don't actually like filling out forms, that they don't even open marketing emails and that they'd much rather buy from people they know than a logo with a cool html template.

None of the plays in this book will scale on their own. And that's exactly why they've helped us cut through the noise, grow faster than our competitors and thrill our customers. Because we don't obsess over scale. We obsess over experience.

One final call-to-action. Obviously, no pretty, well-formatted button you can click. Instead, we'd love to hear from you. **Email us with what you thought of this book**. We'll produce volume two some day and the only way it will be better than this version is if we hear from you.

Sincerely,

The Drift Marketing Team

Dan can be reached at dan@drift.com
Dave can be reached at dg@drift.com
Alex can be reached at aorfao@drift.com
Sara can be reached at spion@drift.com
John can be reached at john@drift.com
Janna can be reached at janna@drift.com

About The Authors

Dave Gerhardt – Dave is currently the VP of Marketing at Drift. Dave was employee number ten at Drift (and the first marketing hire). He is obsessed with building an audience. He is the co-host of Seeking Wisdom which 50,000 people download a month at the time of publishing this book. You can connect with Dave on twitter at @davegerhardt.

Daniel J. Murphy – Daniel is the Director of Product Marketing at Drift. Daniel has worked at several B2B SaaS companies including Onshape and HubSpot in numerous roles including product marketing, marketing ops and demand generation. Daniel is a self proclaimed marketing nerd and loves working with startups. You can connect with Daniel on twitter at @_danieljmurphy.

Sara Pion – Sara is a Growth Marketer at Drift. She started as a customer advocate, helping to create the support team at Drift. Since joining the marketing team, Sara has used her knowledge of the platform to help Drift and customers optimize their usage of the platform to drive ROI. You can connect with Sara on twitter at @sara_pion.

Alex Orfao – Alex is responsible for Drift's email communication strategy and channel marketing efforts. She's been in the B2B SaaS space for 5 years, working in demand generation roles at companies like LogMeIn, HubSpot, Bullhorn and Brightcove. Alex got her job at Drift by responding to an automated marketing email.

John DeWolf – John is a software engineer on the marketing team at Drift. He currently oversees all of marketing's drift.com websites and infrastructure. In John's first two weeks at Drift he completed both the Philadelphia marathon and a website redesign.

Janna Erickson – Janna heads up the event team at Drift. With over 10 years working in events at fast growing companies like HubSpot, Kayak and now Drift, Janna has had a ton of experience pushing the boundaries with live events. She is primarily focused on Drift's annual conference HYPERGROWTH — the fastest growing marketing and sales conference in the world. You can connect with Janna on twitter at @BostonJanna.